Repugnicants

The Wacky World of Republican Politics

Featuring:

Snoot Gingrich, Snit Romney, Run Paul,
P.Rick Perry, Michele Babblethump,
Herman Pizza and Donald Dump

Edited and Curated by

George Won't

Columnist for the *Washington Pissed*

Repugnicants - Version 1.1

Updated: January 5, 2012

Published by:

The Serendipity Publishing Group

Email: info@serendigity.com

© Serendigity Publishing Group, 2012

All Rights Reserved

ISBN-13: 978-1468127225

ISBN-10: 1468127225

To join with other Repugnicant Patriots visit:

www.repugnicance.net

Follow Repugnicants on Twitter @Repugnicance

To order additional copies of this book visit:

www.repugnicants.com

For additional information or

for discounts on bulk orders email:

info@repugnicants.com

Table of Contents

What They're Saying About

Repugnicance

• *Repugnicance* has more bite than a $10 million ad buy. If widely disseminated, it will assure the victory of the Democrats in November 2012.
– Barack Obamma

• *Repugnicance* is the best political parody to come out in years. We will use it as the touchstone of our campaign this Fall.
- David Flouffe

• It's wicked good humor, and chocked full of insight too.
- David Axelrub

• *Repugnicance* is the best book out today on politics. It's got its finger on the pulse of the puffery, the pandering and the political pollution that's filling the airwaves.
- Al Bore

• *Repugnicance* describes in clear and concise babble all BS that Republicans put forth as policy, programs and platitudes.
– Senator John F. Klarity

• Destined to become a classic of political parody.
- The New York Chimes

• If Mark Twain were alive today this is the kind of book he would write.
- USA Tomorrow

• Whoever this George Won't is, he's got the goods on the Repugnicants.
- Dan Blather

• *Repugnicance* captures the ludicrous tone and shriveled spirit of modern day Republicanism.
- Hairy Reed

• Personally I didn't find this book very funny.
- Snit Romney

• Laced with innuendo, factual inaccuracy and hysterical repugnance.
- Snoot Gingrich

• There are three things I didn't like about this book. It was too one sided. It was biased … and … and … I can't remember the third thing. Oops.
- P.Rick Perry

• This book is blasphemy!
- Michele Babblethump

• Just another left leaning hatchet job.
- Hermann Pizza

• Kudos to George Won't for exposing of the gap between the rhetoric and the reality in politics today.
- Good Night Joe

• *Repugnicance* is the McPain straight talk express in book form.
- John McPain

• I've been covering politics for over 30 years and this is the best parody I have ever read … bar none. Spot on!
- Chris Matthoose

• *Repugnicance* is the most insightful book on politics out today. Damn funny too.
- Nancy Peloski

• This book stunk. It's the worst book I ever read. In fact it's the only book I've ever read.

Chattanooga Times Free Press Bennett

- George B. Wush

• I want to know who this guy George Won't is … so I can congratulate him on a pitch perfect impersonation of perhaps the greatest political commentator of our age.
- George Will

• Todd and I are indignant that this book has been published. It's like a voyeur had camped out on our deck and was peering into our bedroom to get our privately, Repugnicant conversations.
- Saint Sarah

• And you thought Sarah Palin was funny. You've got to read this book.
- Tina Flake

• *Repugnicance* captures what core Republicanism is all about. It shows how money rules in politics … it exposes the game for what it is - a game that's rigged through inside deals financed by lobbyists and campaign contributors. It shows how the 1% to get rich at the expense of the 99%. Then I ask myself, what's wrong with all of that?
- Donald Dump

INTRODUCTION BY ANDERSON SCOOPER

I was honored when my colleague, George Won't, asked me to write the introduction to his two seminal works of political satire:
- *Repugnicance: The Wacky World of Republican Politics.*
- *Repugnicance: The 2012 Version of the Republican ~~Bible~~ Babble*

Writing for the *Washington Pissed*, George Won't has long been   at the forefront of the Jugular Journalism Movement.   It comes natural to him because he's one ornery dude. His name says it all. George Won't is a contrary kind of guy. George Won't be a part of the charade of junkfood journalism. George Won't play games with politicians and editors. George Won't is one

tough SOB and he don't take nothing from nobody. George Won't and others are now helping to define a new genre which we might call Occupy Journalism. What's it all about?

Imagine if you were a reporter and could ask anything of the Republican candidates. Imagine if they had no handlers present and were forced to respond to your questions, no matter how impertinent you might be. Imagine if you had the power to force an honest response and honest reaction to probing question. Imagine this and you will imagine what George Won't has done in this pathbreaking parody of the Repugicants.

I won't say that I agree with George Won't on everything. Frankly, I was a little shocked that he was so hard on Snit Romney. I've been covering the Romnoid for a long time and I've never seen Snit so pissed. At one point in that interview, Snit just lost it. I suppose he's entitled to one meltdown in a long and grueling campaign. But, until that incident, it never occurred to me that Snit might be a human being. That's the true value of jugular journalism: you get to see what politicians are really like beneath their veneer.

As for George's treatment of Snoot Gingrich ... well ... Snoot's got it coming to him. I was glad to see George shine some light on the shadiness Snoot's past dealings, his infidelities and his wacky positions. Sooner or later people are going to remember who Snoot really is. I can only hope that the voters catch on, before Snoot ends up in the Whitewash House. I'm glad George Won't had the courage to call Snoot out on all this.

Republicans in general have lost their mooring. There was a time when they stood for something, most notably: fiscal responsibility. Today's Republicans have morphed into something both comically grotesque and grotesquely comic. You have no choice, now, but to call them: Repugnicant - that's a totally repugnant form of Republicanism.

Face it ... the Republican circus this season has been an over-the-top carnival of gaffes. Unfortunately, it also has an ominous quality to it. Today's Republicans are the party of "No." They have no strategic vision to address any of the myriad problems that facing this country. In response to real problems, all we get from Republicans are platitudes, talking points and attacks against  Democratic proposals. It's not a well thought out plan ... or winning strategy. In this pathbreaking book, George Won't lays down the law. George Won't be a part of the hype and hypocrisy that define Republicanism today. This book is a must read for anybody who wants to know what's really happening in politics today – a long steep decline in the quality of public discourse.

THE REPUGNICANT NATIONAL UNCONVENTION

MARK YOUR CALENDAR FOR AUGUST 31 - SEPT 2, 2012

Spliced between the Republican and Democratic Conventions, on the weekend of August 31-Sept 2, 2012, there will be another spectacle called the Repugnicant National Unconvention, taking place on college campuses and select locations around the U.S.A. It will be extremely loosely coordinated by those who **really** don't know what they are doing – the esteemed body aptly dubbed the Repugnicant National Uncommittee. This epochal event will serve as a truly ~~historical~~ hysterical Fall campaign kickoff and an organizing vehicle for something so grand … that … well … even we can't imagine what it might become.

Yes, it's a crazy idea … crazy good. Sometimes crazy is the only appropriate response to a system that has gone crazy on us … as Repugnicance has done. The Repugnicant National Unconvention will be an anti-Republican themed

parody culminating in a theatre of the absurd. Students and other slightly touched participants, will play the roles of Republican caricatures like Snoot Gingrich, Mutt Romney, P.Rick Perry, Run Paul and Donald Dump. These caricatures will go through the motions of selecting a nominee for the Repugnicant Party.

There will be music, skewered speeches, bastardized media interviews in one huge and over-the-top parody of Republicans. It's an Occupy Movement for politics ... political theatre for the Internet age. There will be live Webcasts of campus events, local Repugnicant conventions, all around the country. Facebook groups, Twitter news feeds and YouTube postings and major media outreach. Anyone with a wit and a way can participate. Get creative. Use your wits to register your opposition to politics as usual. Our targets? Whoever and whatever the Republicans put forth as a nominee and a platform.

The buildup to the RNU will continue through the Spring and Summer of 2012 using social networks and YouTube videos, photoshopped images, T-shirts, bumperstickers - all the standard and non standard

paraphernalia of political campaigning.

On this localized, national stage, the RNU will be programmed for viral growth. The disenchanted and disenfranchised can voice their frustrations in a wry way that detracts major media attention. Our goal is to engage the 99%, who are currently left out of the prevailing political equation.

Just like the GOP convention, the RNU will be strong on bombast and political vacuousness. Speakers will mouth political platitudes like they're Repugnicant gospel. Watch crowds will go berserk over the stupidity of self-serving political ~~prophets~~ profits and repugnant media pundits. Sop up the showmanship as if it were real political spectacle. Delegates will cast their votes for the most vapid candidate and we will have accomplished everything that was accomplished at the real Republican National Convention ... nothing at all.

Although whimsical and wacky, the RNU will also have a serious bite . It will expose the current form of Repugnicance as an absurd abstraction – an over the top political philosophy. We'll skewer the Republican candidates by taking Republican ideas to the extreme outer limits of credibility. All in all we'll create a kind of creative dissonance to the Republican National Convention. Save the date, August 31-Sept 1, 2012 and set the stage for the political theatre in its most rapturous and riotous form. Heck, maybe even George B. Wush and Dick Chicanery will come out from their caves to make guest appearances.

REPUGNICANCE MEANS NOT HAVING TO SAY YOU'RE SORRY ... FOR BEING STUPID.

Shakespeare on Repugnicance

To-morrow, and to-morrow, and to-morrow,
Creeps in this petty pace from day to day,
To the last syllable of recorded time;
And all our yesterdays have lighted fools
The way to dusty death.
Out, out, brief candle!
Life's but a walking shadow, a poor player,
That struts and frets his hour upon the stage,
And then is heard no more. It is a tale
Told by an idiot, full of sound and fury,
Signifying nothing.

Macbeth, Act 5, Scene Five

The Early Returns

Iowa Circuses and Hampshire Hoedown

Come the blessed New Year, the Repugnicants' silly season was officially upon us, with the Iowa Circuses and the New Hampshire Hoedown. Taking take a semi-serious look at the candidates and how their campaigns were shaping up, was clearly precarious exercise in a campaign season where all the candidates had their 15 minutes of fame. True to form, yet another emerged from the slumber to steal the spotlight in Iowa.

The ~~Winners~~ Whiners

Rick Snooratrum: The sleeper has awakened ... "Game on!" he says ... casting himself as the "true conservative" in the race ... did he suddenly find his audience .... truly a stunning rise out of nowhere ... leaving him and the rest of the Repugnicants scratching their head ... what did his virtual tie for first place mean for the rest of his campaign ... probably nothing ... no staying power ... perhaps a Vice Presidential nod ... for a semi scary candidate whose "anti-birth control" and neanderthal social stances put him squarely outside of the mainstream ... largely overlooked until now. One thing was for sure ... he'll garnered attention— and serious scrutiny— the fun was just beginning.

Snit Romney: He solidified his underwhelming front-runner status ... the Nott Romney campaign spent over $4 million to damage the Gingrich brand and all he got was a lousy 8 vote win over the suddenly awakened Rick Snooratrum ... his semi-resounding win over the flavor of the week reinforced the "anything but Romney" sentiment for the 2012 version of the Repugnicant roadshow ... Snit's handlers were suddenly talking history ... they said after he wins New Hampshire the dominos in South Carolina and Florida will fall his way ... a January sweep will deliver a knockout punch ... but just to be sure, Snit's handlers bought major media time in South Carolina and Florida ... big picture ... the

Romnoid's semi-success was really a damnation ... in an Evangelical ... ultra conservative field ... but onward ... the Snit started sharpening his rhetorical razor on Obama ... in an Op Ed he wrote: "President Obama wants to change America from an opportunity society to an entitlement society, in which government takes from some to redistribute to others. His aim to create equality of outcomes rather than equality of opportunity." ... Was he having a Snit because he can no longer make due on this millions ... or is it just that he now has so many blind trusts that he can no longer see straight?

Run Paul: The Radical's credentials as a legitimate spoiler were authenticated by the Iowa Circus results ... what's more he had impressive organizations set up in Florida, Idaho and other states ... rabid supporters with online fundraising and Facebook presence second only to the Snit .... the plot sickens ... suddenly the Radical was a real factor in this race ... with proportional voting could end up as the kingmaker in a deadlocked convention.... dare we point out that he's got the same initials as Ross Perot ... Obama's handlers were salivating at the possibilities.

The ~~Losers~~ Laughers

Snoot Gingrich: The Professor officially flamed out in Iowa ... in the breathtaking span of a few weeks ... true to his words he refused to run a negative campaign and instead just laid the truth on the line by calling Snit Romney a liar on national TV ... truly hates the Snit ... he saw Snit bottoming out at 25% ... and himself ... well according to the Professor, he's the only electable alternative ... the professor's always right ... right?

P.Rick Perry: Spent $480 per vote in Iowa ... now that was a Texas size blunder ... When asked how he saw the race

now ... "It's a three horse race ... between Snit Romney, Rick Snooratrum and ... and .... oops ..." One thing's for sure ... the third horse is not him ... he's going back to pasture in Texas. ... but wait ... there's more .... just Tweeted something about South Carolina ... onward and ... and .... and ... and ... oops ..."

Michele Babblethump: Big time loser in Iowa … her candidacy took a sharp U turn after she finished in first place in the Iowa GOP's summer straw poll … after Iowa she stopped thumping her babble … saw no way forward … campaign was out of cash … had been hoping for a fundraising bump from a respectable Iowa finish … instead got a bump in the ass … her conclusion … "Last night, the people of Iowa spoke with a very clear voice, and… I look forward to the next chapter in God's plan." … so sad for the looney lovers … to see Ms. Babblethump stop thumping against Obama care as "the playground of left-wing social engineering" … her 99 country bus tour

Michele Bachmann attempts to eat a foot-long corn dog at the Iowa State Fair

left voters with the same canned stump speech at each stop. … true Repugnicants were sorry to see her go … But the good news is that by only suspending her campaign she could still apply for Federal matching grants to help settle her campaign debts … and still rail against runaway federal spending … like a true Repugnicant.

Donald Dump: Waiting in the wings … we could only hope that by changing his registration from Repugnicant to Independent … he meant business … we can always dream …

Saint Sarah: Oh sweet Sarah where art thou … we all miss thy run on sentences and profound pronouns …

Real Repugnicance

The ultimate objective of all Repugnicance is taking private gain at public expense. This is the real organizing principle of all Repugnicant political activity. True Repugnicants have forged a a convenient but uneasy alliance with various extremist groups in a coordinated effort to broaden the base of support of the 1% that will reap the rewards of Repugnicance. The votes of these extremist groups can be encapsulated in the 5 Gs ... Guns ... anti-Gays ... God ... anti-Government and Gold. The votes of these groups are reliable, since all of these groups are obsessively focused on one issue. True Repugnicants don't really give a rats ass about these issues, but they need the votes of these extremist groups to maintain their power base. In reality, every Repugnicant's political position is underscored by a desire to enrich themselves through government ... cutting taxes ... bailouts ... perks ... government contracts ... regulatory relief ... on and on. These are the real payoffs and objectives of Repugnicance. This is the real profit in Repugnicance. In the following pages the chosen ~~Prophets~~ Profits of Repugnicance blow smoke in the eyes of the electorate, through carefully crafted talking points ... a kind of eloquent babble that conceals their real objective: to profit from the system.

GOD SAVE US
from your followers

THE PROFESSOR

I'M SNOOT GINGRICH AND I DON'T HAVE ... A PRINCIPLE.

The Gospel According to Snoot

Washington Pissed: Speaker Gingrich, you had an affair while you were married and then divorced your first wife while she was dying of cancer saying to a friend and I quote, "She not young enough ... and she's not pretty enough to be the wife of a president ... and besides she has cancer."

Snoot Gingrich: I freely admit that I've made mistakes. I have learned the meaning or repentance. I have repented for marrying that dog. Factually my statement was correct. She did have cancer and she really wasn't very pretty. I'm won't say she was actually ugly ... but...

Washington Pissed: Snoot ... do you hear what you are saying? You're trying to appeal to voters that are strong on family values. What kind of family values does that kind of behavior represent?

Snoot Gingrich: When I left her ... I got married again ... and again ... until I finally got it right. I started another family. This is the American way. I finally got a functional wife ... 20 years younger than me. In a sense that's what America needs to do today. We need a fresh start. When we elected Obama it was a mistake ... a bad marriage. When you make a mistake, you've got to repent and move on. America needs to repent for the sin of electing Obama. I am the candidate of repentance for true conservatives.

Washington Pissed: So you're suggesting it's okay to ditch your wife, especially when she's dying of cancer.

Snoot Gingrich: Hey... She was history. I'm a historian. ... Why waste my time or hers with a lot of feigned sympathy. Turn the page of history.

Washington Pissed: Is that what family values are to you?

Snoot Gingrich: Look at the facts ... over half of Americans get divorced today ... by getting divorced I made my record on marriage acceptable to the majority of Americans.

Washington Pissed: Speaking of your record ... former Speaker Nancy Pelosi says that the Congressional ethics committee has boatloads of dirt on you from your alleged ethics violations while you were speaker of the house. That's a lot of baggage to try to haul all the way to the Presidency.

Snoot Gingrich: Pelosi may have the dirt on me but she can't use it.

Washington Pissed: Why?

Snoot Gingrich: It would be a violation of House ethics rules to disclose that.

Washington Pissed: Say that again...

Snoot Gingrich: The House ethics committee has clear rules ... about exposing the ethics violations of its members.

Washington Pissed: But isn't that why the House has ethics rules in the first place?

Snoot Gingrich: I don't think you quite understand how our government works.

Washington Pissed: Enlighten me.

Snoot Gingrich: Government is all about secrecy. Campaigning is all about giving the appearance of transparency. Governing and campaigning are two different animals entirely.

Washington Pissed: But don't the voters need to know what goes on behind the veil of secrecy so that they can make informed choices about candidates.

Snoot Gingrich: Your naiveté is charming.

Washington Pissed: My naiveté?

Snoot Gingrich: Listen … if voters really knew what was going on, no incumbent would ever be re-elected and our government would constantly be run by a bunch of unseasoned newbies who don't know what they're doing.

Washington Pissed: But isn't that what we have now?

Snoot Gingrich: No, we have a government by people who know what they are doing … but are basically dishonest.

Washington Pissed: So having dishonest politicians is better than incompetent politicians.

Snoot Gingrich: Exactly.

Washington Pissed: But wouldn't a newer crop of politicians eventually learn how the system works?

Snoot Gingrich: Yes, and they'd get corrupted in the process. Why wait ... life's too short ... just like my divorce that you were mentioning earlier.

Washington Pissed: Shifting focus here, Michele Babblethump has criticized you for your lobbying activities ... taking $1.6 million from Fannie Mae ... suggesting that your are the epitome of crony capitalism? Any comment?

Snoot Gingrich: Let me be very clear about this. I have never engaged in lobbying activities.

Washington Pissed: But these entities from which you accepted consulting fees aren't normally known for their charitable tendencies. Surely they expected something in return for what they were giving you.

Snoot Gingrich: Let me repeat ... I have never changed my positions based upon money that I have taken from corporate interests.

Washington Pissed: For you to say this with a straight face is stunning. For someone of your political pedigree, so say something so patently absurd in full public view, shows a level of intellectual dishonesty unrivaled even in the hallowed halls of Repugnicance. Do you expect anyone to believe such openly disingenuous statements?

Snoot Gingrich: The voters will believe anything they're told as long as it's said with an air of authority. That's why I've carefully cultivated my professorial image ... so that my intellectual dishonesty becomes credible to the voters. They even start to see it as an asset rather than a liability.

Washington Pissed: Good point. Everybody talks about how smart you are and how well you handle the attacks from your opponents in the debates. But, do you sometimes have difficulty keeping your various personas straight? You're a professor ... a historian ... a lobbyist ... an author ... a politician? I would think sometimes one persona might flow into another without you're being aware of the transition.

Snoot Gingrich: Very perceptive. Yes I sometimes do have trouble keeping them straight. It taxes my vast intelligence, but fortunately I have plenty of of that to spare.

Washington Pissed: Speaking of your trouble keeping things straight ... how did you end up with a half million dollar tab at Tiffany's?

Snoot Gingrich: Shopping ... how else would I run up a tab of that magnitude?

Washington Pissed: Of course ... my bad ... that makes perfect sense. Is that the same sort of thing as the government running up a $15 trillion dollar tab for our excess borrowing?

Snoot Gingrich: Exactly ... think about it ... what really makes America great these days? Is it manufacturing? ... no we have no manufacturing base these days. Is it our Democracy? No, we have no democracy these days ... Is it great athletes? ... No ... many of our best athletes are most imported from overseas. So what does America do best?

Washington Pissed: Beats me.

Snoot Gingrich: Shopping! We're the best shoppers in the world. When America shops we do it with a vengeance. Look at what happened on Black Friday. If you weren't armed with pepper spray, you were outta luck in the stores. We are the best shoppers in the world because we take our shopping seriously and have the military equipment to back up our desires.

Washington Pissed: So is that why we invest so much money in defense spending?

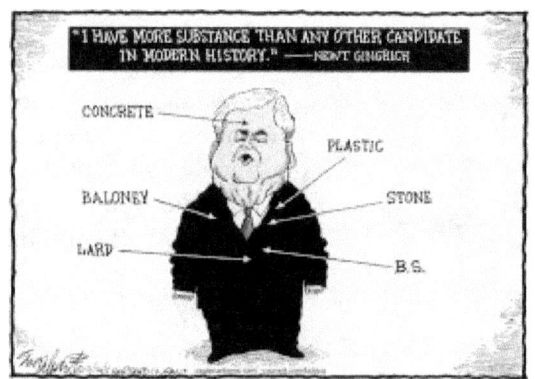

Snoot Gingrich: Exactly ... without that military we wouldn't be able to buy oil on the cheap ... or convince those who are sending us all the cheap goods we import to continue lending to us so that we can feed our appetite for stuff. This is what makes America great these days. We're the envy of the world.

Washington Pissed: Speaking of the rest of the world. You said that the Palestians are an "invented people." What do you mean by that?

Snoot Gingrich: I mean just what I said. Before we invented the Palestinian state, Palestinians were not legitimized. So technically my statement is correct. Palestinians are invented in the sense that their legitimacy is entirely a product of human intervention.

Washington Pissed: But Snit Romney suggests that such statements are inflammatory and could cause tumult in a region of the world that's already powder-keg. Is it responsible for a man who is campaigning to become the most powerful person in the world to make such irresponsible statements?

Snoot Gingrich: There is nothing irresponsible about speaking the truth. Ronald Reagan spoke the truth when he said Russia was an evil empire.

Washington Pissed: Surely you're not implying that you're another Ronald Reagan?

Snoot Gingrich: Well, you have to admit that they're many similarities.

Washington Pissed: Such as?

Snoot Gingrich: For starters, we both ditched our first wives … and we're both great communicators… Did you see my masterful performance in the debates? The list can go on and on. The Repugnicant nomination is all but over … it's history.

Washington Pissed: You're making my head spin. … How do you respond to Snit Romney's point that such statements might inflame the region with even more violence?

Snoot Gingrich: Hey, Snit should talk. He is the ultimate "invented candidate."

Washington Pissed: Explain.

Snoot Gingrich: Who is Snit Romney? Is he a legitimate person. Obviously not. When he decided to run for President, he hired consultants to invent his public persona, crafting policy positions and personality characteristics based on their focus group findings.

Washington Pissed: How does that make him invented?

Snoot Gingrich: Ask yourself, "What is an invention? "An invention is something that is constructed artificially … like a robot … that is what an invention is. Snit Romney is a political robot programmed to behave like the ideal candidate.

Washington Pissed: And you? Have you been invented?

Snoot Gingrich: You can say many things about me … but one thing you cannot say about me is that I've been manufactured or invented. I speak what is on my mind, and for that reason I'm going to be the Republican nominee and next President of The United States. I will change the culture in Washington.

Washington Pissed: But you are the Washington culture personified. How can you convince the voters that someone with so much baggage all acquired through your Washington insider persona, that you're the person to change that culture in Washington, DC?

Snoot Gingrich: Simple. I've got a new Contract on America … It sounds like sweeping change … but is just the same OLE … same OLE. It's Repugnicance to the hilt.

Washington Pissed: Sounds like a winning strategy…. Good luck to you sir … always refreshing to speak with someone so forthright about himself and how the system really works … good to have you with us again at the *Washington Pissed.*

Snoot Gingrich: My pleasure any time.

The Repugnicance Contract on America

ON THE DAY AFTER THE REPUGNICANCE REVOLUTION, WE PROMISE TO:

1. Require all laws that apply to the rest of the country do not apply to Congress;

2. Select a semi-reputable accounting firm to take a cursory glance at what happens behind the doors of Congressional committees and file a report of not less that 100,000 pages written in microscopic font to insure that nobody will read it.

3. Cut three departments from the executive branch of government ... education, interior and .... and ... oops ... where's P.Rick Perry when we need him;

4. Limit the chairs that are used in committee rooms to insure that the press is excluded;

5. Ban the casting of open and transparent votes in Congress;

6. Require committee meetings to be open to all lobbyists and give them first dibs on the empty seats in the room;

7. Require a six-fifths majority vote to pass a tax increase;

8. Guarantee an unusual accounting of the Federal Budget using the latest technology of smoke and mirrors.

THE PANDERER

I'M SNIT ROMNEY

... AND I DON'T HAVE A CONVICTION.

MITT ROMNOID:
A CANDIDATE
WITHOUT A CHARACTER

The Gospel According to Snit

A Candid Interview with Snit Romney
Exclusive to the Washington Pissed

Washington Pissed: Does this interview finally mean that you're warming up to the media?

Snit Romney: Who could ever warm up to the media?

Washington Pissed: Good point. But if you're a candidate, you've got to do it … that is, if want the voters to have some idea of who you really are, beneath your plastic exterior.

Snit Romney: Excuse me? Beneath my plastic exterior?

Washington Pissed: Yeah! Some say that you're afraid that the Romney brand might be damaged by answering real questions about what you really believe and, God forbid, what you really feel. Conservative voters in the primaries might see you're really not a conservative. More liberal voters in the general election might see you're really not a liberal. The net result is that everybody now thinks you don't really have any core convictions and the Romney brand has been irreparably damaged. Any comment?

Snit Romney: I don't know what you mean by the Romney Brand.

Washington Pissed: Yes you do. It's the same brand that your packaging consultants have created. You're being sold to the voters just like the brand of Staples you once helped create with your hard earned Venture Capital at Bain Private Equity. You're being marketed just like

"IT POLLS WELL."

soap. Unfortunately for you the Romney brand isn't washing with the voters. The polls have been sending you a message. The voters want anybody but the Snit. The Romney brand isn't selling well in the marketplace of politics.

Snit Romney: Oh that brand. Why didn't you say so? We'll see whether it washes out. We like the Romney brand. It's an affable brand … it's a clean brand … a consistent brand … a stable brand ...

Washington Pissed: Yes, but it's also the brand that has many people asking, "Who is this guy?" I'm giving you to an opportunity here to consider opening up a bit … to give some nuance to your personality and your policy positions … which I'm sure you admit have on occasion changed a bit.

Snit Romney: My positions haven't changed, since I last changed them.

Washington Pissed: Good point, but the record shows your positions have changed with alarming frequency.

Snit Romney: What record?

Washington Pissed: Your public record.

Snit Romney: My public record no longer exists in public view. Everything I've said in public for the last 20 years has been carefully scrubbed and sanitized to remove any basis for controversy. I even had my staff remove all the hard drives from their computers before I left office in Massachusetts in 2008.

Washington Pissed: Yes, and that raised eyebrows - creating the kind of controversy you were seeking to avoid. You've also refused to release your tax returns and the names of the "bundlers" who raise big bucks for your campaign. This makes you seem controlling and, shall we say, less than transparently human. What are you trying to hide? Is there information here that would damage the Romney brand or expose deep character flaws?

Snit Romney: My allegiance to the principles of Repugnicance demands that I keep both my financial information and my character my flaws hidden from public view.

MITT ROMNOID
A POLITICIAN WITHOUT
A PERSONALITY.

Washington Pissed: Is that why you had the hard drives removed?

Snit Romney: Listen … I don't need to respond to your questions. I'm doing this interview as a favor to you… not because I need it.

Washington Pissed: Do you ever get mad, I mean like really pissed?

Snit Romney: (Silence)

Washington Pissed: Do you have any personality beneath that veneer?

Snit Romney: Personality … what's that?

Washington Pissed: Is there some there there?

Snit Romney: What you're implying is unsupported by the facts.

Washington Pissed: Okay, then, there really is no there, there. So why should anyone vote for you?

Snit Romney: Because my carefully crafted public persona is so well constructed by my team that it's better than the other candidates whose personality flaws have been on full public display. My exterior is impervious to penetration ... the voters have no wiggle room in their thinking about me and reporters have no wiggle room in their interpretation of what I have said.

Washington Pissed: No wiggle room?

Snit Romney: Right ... every time I open my mouth you blowhards say I've just flip flopped.

Washington Pissed: But isn't that what you do?

Snit Romney: No Comment.

Washington Pissed: I see ... you don't want to play. But let's take Obama Care. What do you think of that? Were you for it or against it?

Snit Romney: No Comment.

Washington Pissed: Hello? Earth to a humanoid ... any human trace inside there? Is there anyone inside ... who feels passion about anything? Is there a human being inside who gets angry? Why are you so afraid to show your emotions? Showing emotion just might be the ticket to convincing the voters that you're not a fake. You're getting red in the face now. Are you getting angry that I'm being so honest?

Snit Romney: I'm not angry... I'm just having a snit.

Washington Pissed: Well snit away. Maybe soon we'll find a real person hidden in there. You're actually starting to show some real emotion now. Just out of curiosity, what do Mormon's do when they get mad, since they're not supposed to swear.

Snit Romney: Mormon's discourage swearing, but it's not a covenant. Personally I look at swearing as a loss of self control... not a Mormon dictate. Besides, My Mormon faith is a private matter. It shouldn't be a relevant consideration for the voters.

Washington Pissed: But it is. In fact, many fundamentalist Christians would rather vote for an adulterer like Snoot Gingrich than a Mormon. What do you say to that?

Snit Romney: F...k them!

Washington Pissed: I beg your pardon?

Snit Romney: You heard what I said. F...k them!

Washington Pissed: Oh ... I see where you're headed with this. You're showing everybody your Mormon faith doesn't bind you. But this looks like another flip flop … this one coming at the expense of your Mormon faith. Right?

Snit Romney: Fuck you.

Washington Pissed: You're dark side is coming through now. Is this why your handlers keep you on such a tight leash?

Snit Romney: F...k yeah!

Washington Pissed: There we go … finally we're scratching the beneath the surface … maybe there really is a human being behind the door? Keep it up … the voters are warming up to you now!

Snit Romney: F...k you!

Washington Pissed: We're making real progress now! Can we assume that the real person beneath your highly polished campaign persona feels true passion when he says, "F...k you?"

Snit Romney: F...k yeah!

Washington Pissed: You don't wish to say anything else but F… them ... F…k you, and F..k yeah?

Snit Romney: F...k no!

Washington Pissed: Thank you Governor! It's been a real pleasure getting to know you better. Is this why you don't like to talk to the media?

Snit Romney: F...k this! I'm outta here!

THE CLOWN

I'M P.RICK PERRY
AND I DON'T
... HAVE A BRAIN

The Gospel According to P.Rick

Washington Pissed: Now that you've gone back to Texas, Michele Babblethump has stopped thumping her babble and Herman Pizza's Lametrain has derailed, how do you see the Repugnicant race shaping up?

P.Rick Perry: I see it as a three horse race now. There's Snit Romney. There's ... and there's ... . humm ... Let's see ... There's Snit Romney. There's ... and there's ... . I can't remember ... I know there's a second and third horse in this race ... Oops.

Washington Pissed: Surely Governor you aren't thinking that you're still a serious contender for the Repugnicant nomination.

P.Rick Perry: That's it ... I knew we'd think of the third horse in this race.   .... it's me ... me, myself and .... Wait .... I know there's a third one ... me .... myself and .... I can't think of the third one ... Me ... Myself and .... Oops.

Washington Pissed: Governor, you showed an impressive command of history in the debates, do you think the voters the Iowa circuses sent a message that another Texas shoot 'em up airhead might not be the best thing for our country at this critical juncture in history ... after all ... the last Texas cowboy in the White House didn't work out so well ... any comment?

P.Rick Perry: Which President are you referring to there?

Washington Pissed: Pardon me ... I forgot you didn't do so well in history ... I'm referring to George Bush.

P.Rick Perry: Wasn't he from Connecticut or Massachusetts or one of them Eastern elite states?

Washington Pissed: No ... I'm referring to George W. Bush ... the son...

P.Rick Perry: There were two of them?

Washington Pissed: Surely you remember. Aren't you a Christian?

P.Rick Perry: Of course I'm a Christian. What do you mean?

Washington Pissed: Well in the Republican Babble, it is written ... first the father ... then the son.... then the ...

P.Rick Perry: Oh I get your drift ... then the holy ghost ... in the White House ... that would be me. Right?

Washington Pissed: God willing... You are the holy one aren't you? Would you like to talk about your faith credentials? We know it's coming... so we might as well get it out of the way now.

P.Rick Perry: Thank you for asking ... yes ... well, God and I have a very close relationship. Whenever we've got something to say to each, other I just pick up the spirit phone in my heart and talk to the Almighty. The line's never busy.

Washington Pissed: Are you saying that your faith is stronger than the faith of others in the Presidential Race ... unnamed candidates who might not practice your form of Christian faith?

P.Rick Perry: There are Christians ... true Christians ... and then there are the other cults.

Washington Pissed: Are you suggesting that Mormonism isn't a Christian faith?

P.Rick Perry: I'm not suggesting it. I'm sayin' it! In Texas we don't mince words.

Washington Pissed: Speaking of not mincing words ... you had some pretty strong words of Fed Chairman Ben Bernanke ... saying that if he came down to Texas you would treat him "ugly." What did you mean by that?

P.Rick Perry: What do you think I meant?

Washington Pissed: Are you talking about a lynching?

P.Rick Perry: A lynching wouldn't go far enough for that treasonous ...

Washington Pissed: Hold it ... what else could you do to him? He's the most influential financial figure in the world.... and in this world money talks.

the shadow knows!

P.Rick Perry: In Texas we speak a different language.

Washington Pissed: Are you saying that in Texas money doesn't talk. Seems to me that money has spoken pretty convincingly to you in your appointments as Governor. At last count there were two gazillion political appointments during your tenure as Governor – all based primarily on how much money they gave you or your campaigns.

P.Rick Perry: Is there another criteria for political appointments?

Washington Pissed: Some people think that competence might sometimes be a relevant consideration.

P.Rick Perry: Hey, don't go Eastern snob on me. Just cause I'm an Aggie don't mean I don't got all the goods … mental wise.

Washington Pissed: Then how do you explain your mental lapses in the debates?

P.Rick Perry: It's all part of the image thing. I don't want the come across to the voters as smug or superior, like Snoot 'n Snit.

Washington Pissed: No worries about that! But surely you're not serious.

P.Rick Perry: I'm dead serious. I make the voters feel superior to my mental capabilities. It's my way of showing my respect for the voters and their intelligence.

Washington Pissed: I see … so you make the voters feel smart by appearing to be stupid?

P.Rick Perry: Bingo!

Washington Pissed: So then … to review … are you smart for appearing stupid? … or stupid for now appearing smart?

P.Rick Perry: You lost me on that one.

Washington Pissed: That's okay. You just answered my question. Shifting horses here in mid interview… who does your hair?

P.Rick Perry: Glad you asked about that… It's all natural … no creams … no oil slick in my hair… in Texas oil comes from the ground and goes into pipes not into the hair.

Washington Pissed: Speaking of oil … some people think that your policies are crafted to appeal to what is already the biggest and most obscenely profitable industry in the world … and that you'll do everything in your power as President to make them even richer.

P.Rick Perry: Damn right I will …
and once Texas has all the money we'll secede from the union and colonize the rest of the United States.

Washington Pissed: Colonize?

P.Rick Perry: Yep … just like the British did with the new world … until the American Revolutionaries turned things upside down. We're the new revolutionaries … that's why I supported the Tea Party in the 13th century and I support them now.

Washington Pissed: The 13th century?

P.Rick Perry: Yes that's when the Tea Party dumped the coffee in the ocean.

Washington Pissed: Wasn't that tea?

P.Rick Perry: Oops … my bad.

Washington Pissed: What's next for the Perry campaign? You've raised a ton of money … but you're campaign seems dead in the water. How are you going to spend all that money you raised. You spent $480 per vote in Iowa, how else can you waste that money?

P.Rick Perry: Well we're going to waste that money by letting the people know about the real P.Rick Perry, and building the base for my 2016 run. Have you seen the storyboards for my 2016 ads?

Washington Pissed: No, I can't wait. Can you give me a sneak preview?

P.Rick Perry - A Natural Born Leader

Those of us who grew up with P.Rick in Paint Creek, Texas recall the day we know'd he's a natural born leader. It was the day, that Barb Nabors brought in a new set of utensils to the Squat n Gobble. Till then, for the rest of us locals, our hands was all we needed to stuff food in our mouths. But word had gotten out about how utensils, made everything a lot less messy and saved on laundry bills for the napkins.

As Mama passed around the knives and forks, most of us at the table just looked at em like, "Yeah, so now what ... how do we used these new fangled things?"

Not P.Rick. He picked em up and knew which end to hold and how to jam 'em into the food so that they could lift things. We watched in awe.

From that moment, we know'd that P.Rick had something that none of the rest of us had. It was like he'd been anointed to use those utensils by God himself. That's what leadership is all about. P. Rick is a natural born leader. From that day on, Paint Creek was never the same. P.Rick was like the hundredth monkey. Pretty soon everybody was using utensils and the story of how P.Rick changed our world became part of the legend of The Amazing P.Rick Perry. The legend is still growing to this day. Course now and then he goes back to the old way ... old habits is tough to break, 'specially when the food not on the fork is a hot dog.

P.Rick Perry - The True Christian

Recently, you may have been hearing a lot in the media about the debate

dustup between P.Rick and that Mormon.

Some people have intimidated that our P.Rick has gone aggressive on em. And why shouldn't he? The other inferior religion of an unmentioned Presidential Candidate from Massachusetts, deserves a good ole Texas whooping. Some say P. Rick has amped up his attacks just to provoke media wordage ... drudging up ghosts and God knows what all.

Do not be deceived by they're saying about P.Rick in the other cults! P.Rick is an officially registered Christian. P.Rick's commitment to God almost predates the Babble itself. We have been practicing his faith for eons and pretty soon he expects to get it right. P.Rick ain't prone to flip flopping, political finger in the wind ... focus grouped massaging of message that other candidates pay powerful big bucks to invent on the spur of the moment to appeal to the constituency du jour. In point of fact, we strongly suspect and can prove (beyond all suspicion) that some members of the media may have planted ridicule on the authentication of P.Rick's evangelical credentials. But it didn't work!

All of this would not surprise us given the cutthroat shenanigans that tend to pervade the crazy world of politics and its environs. Sometimes professorial types like Snoot 'n Snit get all uppity in the debates, but J. Rick ain't one of them. He leans on his hard work, not fancy verbiage and lift himself up by the bootstraps to live the American dream. In America anything is possible and we don't hold a grudge against other Christian pretenders to authentic evangelism who might choose to be members of cult religions just because that's what they're all about. Did you get my point?

Rick Perry - The Real Deal

First off we want to set the record straight about J. Rick. The media whores seem not to understand his makeup and I ain't talkin' about cosmetics. J. Rick ain't one for puffery. Authentic Christian he is. This has not been easy to convey to non believers, especially given J. Rick's tendency for gab libbin. Okay, in his book Fed UP, maybe the fonts we used wasn't small enough for their glasses to see clearly and therefore beneath their dignity to read without getting snooty.

The real reason we want to go on the record is to put to rest the notion that P.Rick is a clown and his campaign is a cosmic joke.

Not! P.Rick is the real deal? He may even be the authentic second coming of somebody who is truly a person worthy of note and special attention that he has warranted from the mainstream press not withstanding the rot that spews forth from the media pundits? You decide!

Nuff said.

An Honest Politician - Not a Slick Debater

"Up Yours," snotty syntax vigilantes. If P.Rick's wordage ain't up to your Ivy League admission standards then stuff it! P.Rick Perry is an Aggie and proud of it. Aggies ain't all that big on fancy verbiage and lot's of pusilinamous punctuation. What matters to P.Rick is meaning, not the words he chooses to convey it. To put it another way, he ain't no Shakespeare. He comes from a place on the earth where people are people ... not assholes.

P.Rick Perry is a doer ... not a talker or a whiner.

To write his seminal book, Fed Up, P.Rick worked with an East Coast, erudition expert taking a crash course in wordage and beefed up writing so his word slippage wouldn't be quite so apparent. He tried out the erudition language for a ride around the ranch, and it just weren't for him. P.Rick prefers straight talk to pomposity.

Okay, now and then in the debates he may have inserted less than optimal word usage and had a mental lapse or two. But out on the campaign trail, he talks with gusto. Did you see that speech in New Hampshire, where he was so powerful, folks thought he was high. P.Rick just can't be cut out for what he weren't meant to be and that's the way it is.

Sure he's got some mental constraints, but inside the gut is what counts in a person and it's there that P.Rick shines, even if the words he uses don't always show it.

THE LOONEY

I'M MICHELE BABBLETHUMP

... AND I DON'T HAVE A CLUE.

The Gospel According to Saint Michele

Washington Pissed: Let me cut right through the quick here. There are many people who think you're a bit looney. Any comment?

Michele Babblethump: Why would anybody think that?

Washington Pissed: Not sure, but I think it might have something to do with what you say ... and the look in your eyes when you say it.

Michele Babblethump: Sorry if speaking the truth offends people, but that's who I am. I speak the truth no matter who it offends.

Washington Pissed: What if the person it hurts is you?

Michele Babblethump: How could it possibly hurt me?

Washington Pissed: For starters ... look at what happened in Iowa. Not a strong showing for somebody who just last Summer won the Iowa straw poll. What are your plans now?

Michele Babblethump: Now that I've suspended my campaign, I plan to continue speaking the truth.

Washington Pissed: Speaking of the truth ... you've spoken out strongly against the runaway federal spending and the budget deficits ... but, you've only suspended your campaign ... which means that you can still apply for Federal matching grants to help you pay off your campaign debts. How is that consistent with your constant railing against federal spending?

Michele Babblethump: It's entirely consistent ...

Washington Pissed: How?

Michele Babblethump: Please don't push me on specifics now ... I'm really tired after speaking the truth so much.

Washington Pissed: I'm sure you do mean to speak the truth but if we're going to reduce the deficits then... but something has to be cut ... something specific ... entitlements ... health care ... social security ... defense spending ... what specifically would you cut?

Michele Babblethump: I'd cut taxes.

Washington Pissed: But wouldn't that increase the deficits?

MICHELE
BACHMANN

I Stole This Jacket
From A Flight Attendant

MY STORY

Michele Babblethump: No ... you're not listening. Supply side economics is the gospel of Repugnicance ... When supply side economics was born ... it was like the Christ child had been born ... Repugnicants everywhere were given new life ... we were freed from the constraints of logic.

Washington Pissed: Explain...

Michele Babblethump: Listen ... I'm a lawyer by training. Only lawyers can understand the simple truth that the relativity of logic is the the true light for people who don't understand the facts. You only rely on logic when the facts fail you ... at that rapturous moment logic doubles back upon itself, does a complete reversal and starts moving towards your own ends.

Washington Pissed: Marvelous...

Michele Babblethump: It is marvelous! That's the magic in Repugnicance. That's what Repugnicance is all about: magical faith. In the end it's all about faith. You just have to believe what you believe is true and then the facts don't matter any more. It's like the story of the Christ child ... because devout Christians believe it is true, then we can truly understand the facts ... how a star in the sky guided the three wise men hundreds of miles to a manger where the Christ chid of Supply Side economics was born.

Washington Pissed: So that's what supply side economics is all about. I never got it before. Now I do. It's just twisted logic that doubles back on itself and starts moving towards your own ends?

Michele Babblethump: No you weren't listening to what I meant to say.

Washington Pissed: Okay then, what did you mean to say?

Michele Babblethump: I didn't say it...

Washington Pissed: You didn't say what?

Michele Babblethump: I didn't say what you were thinking I said.

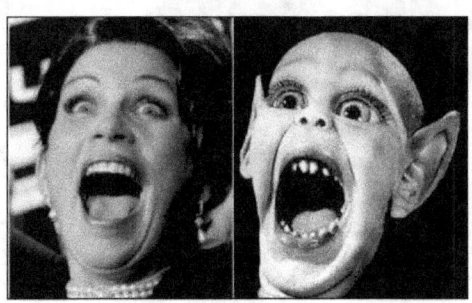

Washington Pissed: You're getting that look in your eyes again.

Michele Babblethump: Yes, it's because I've beheld the rapture.

Washington Pissed: What rapture?

Michele Babblethump: The rapture of the new savior.

Washington Pissed: Don't tell me... the savior of Repugnicant logic.

Michele Babblethump: I didn't say that ... you did. You have seen the light. Now behold the rapture.

THE RADICAL

I'M RUN PAUL
... AND I DON'T HAVE
A PRAYER.

The Gospel According to Saint Paul

Washington Pissed: Your poll numbers suggest that you've got a firm base of rabid supporters, but you can't seem to move beyond that small group of voters. Many commentators describe your rabid followers as "radicals." Are you the radical in the race?

Run Paul: If it's radical to be right then I guess I'm a radical.

Ron Paul at Minneapolis Fed August 31, 2008

Washington Pissed: Okay, let's look at some of these positions where you say you're right and others say you're radical. How about abolishing the Fed? Is that position radical or right?

Run Paul: It's both. The Fed is the antithesis of Democracy. It's gotten us $15 trillion worth of debt which we're going to be passing onto our children and our grandchildren.

Washington Pissed: How is that the antithesis of Democracy?

Run Paul: The citizens have no oversight of what the Fed does. They make decisions behind closed doors and even Congress can't get a peek inside, until they've made their decisions.

Washington Pissed: How is that different from the way other decisions are made in government?

Run Paul: The difference is that with Congress, if the voters don't like the way their representatives are acting they can vote them out of office.

Washington Pissed: But the voters don't know enough about their representatives to decide whose really being honest and whose not.

Run Paul: We're all dishonest and the voters know that. Our approval rating are less than 20%. So voters only approve of one if five of their elected representatives in Congress ... tops.

Washington Pissed: Yet, you're in Congress and you expect voters to vote you into office as President.

Run Paul: I'm the one in five, because I speak the truth.

Washington Pissed: But because you're speaking the truth, the media casts you as a radical, and nobody listens to you.

Run Paul: My rabid supporters listen to me.

Washington Pissed: Oh yes, we forgot about them.

Run Paul: So how will you and your rabid supporters mount a credible campaign for President? Do you have a prayer of winning the nomination?

Washington Pissed: I don't have to win the Republican nomination to have an impact on policy.

Run Paul: Are you suggesting that you might run as a third party candidate?

Washington Pissed: I'm not suggesting anything … other than what I'm suggesting.

Run Paul: So you're going to keep running … no matter what happens?

Washington Pissed: Hey, I'm 77 years old and I've been running for President forever. Forever is a long time.

Run Paul: Is forever long enough for an extreme radical to be taken seriously in the midst of the rest of the Republican babble.

Washington Pissed: You better hope so or we're screwed.

Run Paul: Why do you say that?

Washington Pissed: Because we are screwed. The United States thinks it can continue to be the cop on the beat for the entire world. But to finance our military we have to borrow money from China and other nations that are beginning to wonder whether they should continue lending to us.

Run Paul: And if they finally decide to stop lending to us?

Washington Pissed: We're screwed.

Run Paul: You just said that.

Washington Pissed: Yes and I'll say it again, "We're screwed."

Run Paul: So what's your plan to address that issue.

Washington Pissed: My plan?

Run Paul: Do you have any plan to address the problems that you say are the undoing of the United States?

Washington Pissed: For starters I'd abolish the Fed.

Run Paul: That'll be good. What will that accomplish other than a complete meltdown of the global economy?

Washington Pissed: It will eliminate the $15 trillion in national debt.

Washington Pissed: Then what?

Run Paul: We'll start over again, with a clean slate and no debt.

Washington Pissed: Okay … and how exactly will that work?

Run Paul: We'll have to work out the details. We'll have a lot of time to figure things out because the economy will collapse … there will be no jobs and nobody will be working in the interim.

Washington Pissed: I see, and by then, you'll probably be over a hundred years old.

Run Paul: Yes and I'll be six feet under. I'll enjoy listening to the sound of everybody freaking out above my grave.

THE SLEEPER

I'M RICK SNOORATRUM

... AND I JUST WOKE UP.

The Gospel According to Saint Rick

Washington Pissed: Where did you come from in Iowa? How come nobody noticed you until the vote?

Rick Snooratrum: I was there all along ... practicing politics the old way ... retail politics ... holding town meetings ... driving around the state in my Chuck Truck.

Washington Pissed: So does this mean that the voters have rejected the politics of big money?

Rick Snooratrum: In Iowa it does.

Washington Pissed: In 2007 you called Mormonism a "dangerous cult." Do you stand by those words now?

Rick Snooratrum: I stand by those words, but not if it means I might have to give up the chance of being the Vice President.

Washington Pissed: Spoken like a true Christian conservative who wants a future in politics.

Rick Snooratrum: I plan to continue speaking the truth.

Washington Pissed: You've been outspoken about contraception saying it's against the "natural" way of things. What do you mean by this?

Rick Snooratrum: Hey, if God wants you and your lawfully wedded wife to conceive than you should let God have his way.

Washington Pissed: But what if the circumstances might not be right for bringing a child into the world … say the two partners to sex aren't married.

Rick Snooratrum: Then that's a sin … and God will punish the sinners?

Washington Pissed: How?

Rick Snooratrum: By giving them a child.

Washington Pissed: So childbirth is a form of punishment?

Rick Snooratrum: Of course it is … if the parents aren't responsible Christians.

Washington Pissed: And what does it mean to be responsible Christians?

Rick Snooratrum: It means respecting the Ten Commandments.

Washington Pissed: And what about Mormons… are they responsible Christians.

Rick Snooratrum: Of course not … unless the person practicing Mormonism happens to be the Repugnicant nominee for President who is looking for a good Vice-Presidential candidate who can appeal to evangelicals.

Washington Pissed: Somebody like you?

Rick Snooratrum: You said that, I didn't.

Washington Pissed: Pleasure to have you with us.

Rick Snooratrum: Any time.

THE VICTIM

I'M HERMAN "LAMETRAIN" PIZZA ... AND I DON'T HAVE A CAMPAIGN.

The Gospel According to The Godfather

Washington Pissed: Well you finally done it. You dropped out of the race? Why?

Herman "Lametrain" Pizza: I'm a victim of a media witch hunt. I didn't do anything wrong, but everybody now thinks I did. To put int another way, the media put some unsavory toppings on Herman's Pizza.

Washington Pissed: Too many anchovies ... so to speak?

Herman "Lametrain" Pizza: No it was the pepperoni. Pepperoni was applied in excess.

Washington Pissed: Speaking of excess, apparently you were a bit of a big spender ... lavishing gifts and cash payments to various women in your life ... who it just so happened turned out to be ... not your wife.

Herman "Lametrain" Pizza: You might think of the gifts as anchovies and the cash payments as pepperoni ... without that life is just crust and cheese.

Washington Pissed: So tell me ... what did you say to your wife when you finally faced her ... after your accusers went public?

Herman "Lametrain" Pizza: I asked her where my clothes were?

Washington Pissed: What did she say?

Herman "Lametrain" Pizza: She said, "The emperor has no clothes." I packed them all into suitcases and shipped them off to goodwill.

Washington Pissed: Is that all she said?

Herman "Lametrain" Pizza: No ... she said she'd also sold my cars and then handed me a $20 bill.

Washington Pissed: Why $20?

Herman "Lametrain" Pizza: She said that's all she could get for the cars, "Kinda fire sale," she said without a hint of remorse.

Washington Pissed: So is your campaign now in fire sale mode. I wonder who the lucky buyers will be for your former supporters?

Herman "Lametrain" Pizza: Maybe Snoot Gingrich... We met last week. He made a nice offer ... but the auction is still open. I'm open to all bidders. Snit might submit a winning bid ... He's got a lot of campaign cash and doesn't know what to do with it now that his campaign has tanked. On the other hand, Snoot is now running a bare bones campaign and doesn't have a lot of money for transportation ... so he might buy the rest of my cars.... so to speak.

Washington Pissed: Yes, I know he spent all his spare cash at Tiffanies.

Washington Pissed: How much did Snoot offer?

Herman "Lametrain" Pizza: $10 million up front and then 25% of the proceeds from the sale of the first 25 ambassadorships.

Washington Pissed: Nice offer. Did you take it?

Herman "Lametrain" Pizza: Hey, I'm a businessman. Does a bear shit in the woods? ... I've got a habit and I need money to support it.

Washington Pissed: A habit?

Herman "Lametrain" Pizza: You know...

Washington Pissed: Speaking of... um... habits and women... have you met with The Donald to discuss you post campaign plans.

Herman "Lametrain" Pizza: Yes, we had pizza in Times Square along with Saint Sarah.

Washington Pissed: What did you discuss?

Herman "Lametrain" Pizza: The Donald wants to have a new reality TV show about former Presidential candidates. It's going to be kind of a cross between Survivor, The Apprentice and West Wing.

Washington Pissed: Why would anybody want to watch washed up candidates slug it out all over again?

Herman "Lametrain" Pizza: Beats me. I never understood why anybody would watch the Repugnicant debates either. Apparently he's got sponsors lined up at the door.

Washington Pissed: Like who?

Herman "Lametrain" Pizza: Godfather Pizza for starters.

Washington Pissed: So what's the premise of the show?

Herman "Lametrain" Pizza: Apparently we're all going to be shipped to a faraway island with nothing of the island except lobbyists and hookers. But only one lobbyist has keys to the kingdom and only one hooker has a tattoo on her you know what. The first one of us to both get the keys to the kingdom and find the tattoo wins. Everybody else gets fired.

Washington Pissed: What do you win?

Herman "Lametrain" Pizza: The 2016 Repugnicant Presidential nomination. The Donald will see to that.

Washington Pissed: Oh, I can now see the appeal of the show ... especially for the participants.

Herman "Lametrain" Pizza: In the final episode we're going to get up on a stage and start dancing with the stars.

Washington Pissed: Stars ... like who?

Herman "Lametrain" Pizza: No no, not celebrities ... stars ... like Neptune ... Mars and Pluto.

Washington Pissed: I can see Michele Babblethump really getting into that scene. She's way up there in planetary rotation already. Shifting gears ... will you still push for your 999 plan, even though you're no longer a candidate?

Herman "Lametrain" Pizza: Sort of …. I'm amending it slightly …. After I'm out of the public limelight I'll be pushing for the 696969 plan.

Washington Pissed:
How will that work?

Herman "Lametrain" Pizza: Quite nicely. Now that I'll have the stature of an ex candidate and tons of cash after I sell my support to the highest bidder.

Brainwashed

Washington Pissed:
What if Donald Dump decides to run? Do you think he'd be willing to buy your support?

Herman "Lametrain" Pizza: He's not going to run.

Washington Pissed: But he's threatened to run if the "right" candidate doesn't get the nomination.

Herman "Lametrain" Pizza: Think about it. It's a two horse race now … the Snoot 'n Snit show. Snoot's the brains. Snit's got the bucks. You know who's going to win that race every time. Whoever wins will invite Donald Dump into the White House as an ex-officio member of government.

Washington Pissed: Ex-officio member?

Herman "Lametrain" Pizza: Yeah … it's all part of the grand Repugnicant plan to privatize government.

Washington Pissed: Explain.

Herman "Lametrain" Pizza: Well for example … The next Repugnicant President will put U. S. Congress up for sale. Donald Dump buys it and renames it the National Dumpster…. that's just the beginning. For the right price I'll buy the Washington Monument and rename it in my honor. … something like, "The Leaning Tower of Hermann's Pizza."

Washington Pissed: Quite innovative… especially for Repugnicants. I can also see how that will advance your 696969 initiative.

THE EGO

I'M DONALD DUMP
... AND I DON'T HAVE A COMB.

The Gospel According to The Donald

Washington Pissed: To begin, how do you feel about people referring to you as "The Donald?"

Donald Dump: I feel it's a term of respect. I think people recognize that because I've been enormously successful as a business man ... and my financial statements show that I'm worth over $7 billion ... that I'm due more respect than others in our society who haven't been as smart and successful as I am.

Washington Pissed: Kind of like they've put you on a pedestal.

Donald Dump: Yes, and I deserve to be on a pedestal. I'm thinking of having Donald Dump Pedestals installed at the entrances to my properties ... my hotels in Las Vegas, my condo projects in Florida ... my palace on Fifth Avenue in New York City ... all these owned by me, The Donald. There will be a bust of me combing my hair back with a wave to the masses. I think it would be a nice touch, don't you?

Washington Pissed: Yes, ... I totally agree ... a very sweet and sincere gesture to all the little people who so look up to you as their master. Although I might suggest that instead of inscribing these pedestals with the word, "The Donald" you might consider using "The Dump."

Donald Dump: I don't find that amusing.

Washington Pissed: Oh it wasn't meant to be amusing … it was meant to go deeper than … to penetrate and hopefully puncture your gigantic ego.

Donald Dump: My ego? What exactly are you referring to there?

Washington Pissed: I'm referring to that huge metaphorical blimp that floats above your twisted logic in everything you do and say in life.

Donald Dump: Excuse me! Okay, so I might be a tad self promotional. But success is all about marketing and if you've got something as powerful as my persona to market … hey, why hold back? I've always subscribed to Mae West's philosophy, "If you've got it flaunt it."

Washington Pissed: That you have done. But let's move precariously forward into your thoughts about the Repugnicant candidates for President. Are you satisfied with the current crop of candidates?

Donald Dump: Who could be satisfied when I'm not in the field?

Washington Pissed: So you're still threatening to throw your ego into the ring?

Donald Dump: I don't make idle threats. This is a real possibility that depends on how the nomination process unfolds.

Washington Pissed: Unfolds? What are you saying here?

Donald Dump: I'm saying it depends on whether I can buy the right candidate for the right price.

Washington Pissed: Who is the right candidate?

Donald Dump: I am?

Washington Pissed: So you're going to buy yourself?

Donald Dump: I don't have to buy myself. I already own myself. That's the beauty of my possible campaign. I will already own the candidate.

Washington Pissed: But polls show that for some strange reason the voters might not see "The Donald" as the most qualified or appealing candidate.

Donald Dump: I've considered that.... and so that's why I'm shopping for another one.

Washington Pissed: Shopping?

Donald Dump: Yes, kicking the tires so to speak.

Washington Pissed: Have you found a model that you like?

Donald Dump: At some point I will endorse someone, but not before he's signed the papers.

Washington Pissed: Signed the papers?

Donald Dump: Yes the purchase agreement.

Washington Pissed: And what are the terms of that agreement?

Donald Dump: First and foremost they have to be able to produce a birth certificate. That's mandatory. Beyond that there are pretty standard clauses that we using with the members of Congress that we buy?

Washington Pissed: Such as?

Donald Dump: Boilerplate stuff ... 5 million gets me this ... $10 million gets me that ...

Washington Pissed: Well let's talk about some of the models. How about Sarah Palin?

'You're fired!'

Donald Dump: A very classy chassis.... but she's now a used car.

Washington Pissed: How about Snit Romney?

Donald Dump: Good looking contours ... square jaw ... good hair telegenic ... but there's nothing under the hood.

Washington Pissed: What about Run Paul?

Donald Dump: He's vintage Chevrolet with big fins .... but only appealing to a very small segment of the population ... a niche model.

Washington Pissed: How about Jon Stuntman?

Donald Dump: He's a Mini ... very well designed and engineered ... but you can't fit anything else inside cabin... I don't travel light you know.

Washington Pissed: Yes, we're aware of that? How about Michele Babblethump?

Hairbrained

Donald Dump: Nice body … but the engine kept sputtering … high maintenance vehicle… I'm not a mechanic … when I buy a car I want it to run smoothly … She drove her campaign right into a ditch.

Washington Pissed: So then how about Snoot Gingrich? He seems determined to prove he knows something other people don't know.

Donald Dump: He's a font of ideas. I like that. The big question is all the baggage he's got in the trunk … If we can find a way to toss off all that excess weight he might be the model I'm willing to drive. Too early to tell.

Washington Pissed: Rick Snooratrum?

Donald Dump: Who?

Washington Pissed: He's the sleeper ... your remember ... only lost by 8 votes to Snit Romney in Iowa.

Donald Dump: I guess guess I overslept that morning. I'll have to check him out.

Washington Pissed: Then of course there's P.Rick Perry?

Donald Dump: Yes, I liked him for about 10 minutes ... He's a Toyota pickup. Good if all you want to drive around the ranch and yell "yee haw." other wise, useless. I guess he's going back to his Texas pasture now.

REPUGNICANCE MEANS NOT HAVING TO SAY YOU'RE SORRY ... FOR BEING RICH.

THE HAS-BEEN

I'M GEORGE B. WUSH
... AND I DON'T HAVE A JOB.

The Gospel According to King George

Editors Note: – Some still wonder about the enduring legacy of George B. Wush? At the Repugnicant National Uncommittee we recognize his unique ability to see the world clearly through his own eyes despite having a somewhat obscured perspective. It was a testimony to his political vision and courage that he stuck his head out and in.

GEORGE W. BUSH

SEEING THINGS FROM GEORGE'S POINT OF VIEW

Washington Pissed: So now you're looking out upon at the Repugnican contest from afar. What are your thoughts?

George B. Wush: My thoughts?

Washington Pissed: Yes, what are you thinking?

George B. Wush: Thinking?

Washington Pissed: You do that sometimes, don't you?

George B. Wush: Not if I don't have to?

Washington Pissed: Sorry I didn't mean to intrude on the Zen bliss of your retirement. Let me tact a bit here. I understand that you're writing your memoirs now. Can you give us a glimpse of what might be in this literary masterpiece?

George B. Wush: As you know, I've never been one for wordage. So writing my memoirs ... has been a bit of a mental exercise for me. But fortunately I've got a team of professional writers and editors who follow me around recording what comes out of my mouth ... be it words or sometimes full sentences and they're kind of splicing it all together. They tell me its all coming together quite nicely.

Washington Pissed: How about Laura. She used to be a librarian. Has she been helping in this process?

George B. Wush: Laura is very good organizing books that have already been written so to speak. But writing them is another matter ... especially when the book she is writing is really not the book she is writing ... since it's my book. Do you get my drift?

Washington Pissed: I think so ... not sure really ... but let's move on. Have you watched any of the Repugnicant debates?

George B. Wush: I think I watched the one where P.Rick Perry could remember the third thing ... which I can't remember either. But I think it was a good idea ... eliminating all those parts of the government, even if it's only two.

Washington Pissed: Do you remember anything else?

George B. Wush: I remember the Texas Rangers blowing the World Series agin. Is that what you're talking about?

Washington Pissed: No actually I'm talking about politics, not baseball. The debates ... you know ... with candidates ... questions ... policy positions ... stuff like that. Is this making any sense to you?

George B. Wush: No? I stopped following politics years ago ...

'Are you sitting down?'

Washington Pissed: Back when you were in the Oval Office?

George B. Wush: Was it oval? ... I can't remember... that was so long ago?

Washington Pissed: Thankfully yes ... so very very long ago.

The Book of Jeb

In the Republican ~~Bible~~ Babble the story is told of a God fearing man named Jeb. Jeb had it all:

- Jeb had lots of money and stock options.
- Jeb had a quasi-beautiful wife and semi-sweet children.
- Jeb had smarts, good looks and a bright political future.
- Jeb had name recognition and a legacy - a father who had been ruler of the land.
- Jeb had a network of business and political contacts that was the envy of the world.
- Jeb had campaign contributors coming out the wazoo.

It seemed the crown was Jeb's for the taking. But the Lord did smite Jeb down. Instead of tapping Jeb, the Lord anointed his brother as King George and history may never recover. Jeb suffered through those years even though he had delivered the crucial electoral votes from his state to the promised land of political oblivion.

This was the downfall of Jeb. Soon Jeb's reputation had plunged in market value. His family name no longer had any trading value on the campaign contributory exchange. His credibility had gone kaput, buckling under the weight of his brother's incompetence, incoherence, imbalance and stupidity.

Poor Jeb. All Repugnicants can identify with his sorry plight. Now stuck in the land of palm trees, spoiled fruit and nutcakes, he has no place to go but the beaches where the hot afternoon sun beats down on his future removing any traces of what might have been.

THE REST OF THE REPUGNICANT REGIME

ABCD News - Imbalanced reporting by bloated junkfood journalists who worship at the corporate alter of Mickey Mouse and Donald Duck.

Alan Greenback – Former Chief of Federal Reserve Bored who is plotting with Wall Street wizards and OBooma boosters to develop a plan to negate the national debt with help from the Congress that so assiduously created the immoral debt in the first place without a passing thought to the interests of future generations of Americans who are not represented by their representatives.

Bill O'Really O'Reilly? – Foxy News Network talking head who flagellates guests on his show with hardball questions and then interrupts so fast that the guest becomes whooped ever before they open their mouth. His favorite line ... "Shut up." O'Really? ... Oh O'Reilly!

Condolessa Nice – Former national security advisor and Secretary of State who tried to bring a feminine perspective to the George B. Wush inner circle. But she is now off into his own world of hobnobbing with old boy networks, which he is not one, being a woman.

Christine O'Donnell – Tea Party favorite who snatched defeat from the jaws of victory as a Delaware Senatorial hopeful, helping the Democraps to retain control of the U. S. Senate. Recently tossed her coveted endorsement towards Snit Romney, thereby assuring him of winning "the Witch" vote.

Dan Quail – Dim witted, former VEEP, famed for his deer-in-the-headlights look when reporters asked questions. Today a private equity magnate.

Dick Chicanery – Smiley faced former VEEP who was asked to find the perfect running mate for George W. Bush and instead picked himself. For 8 long years he served as defacto President while holding down a second job as full-time lobbyist for Halliburton Corporation. A man with a mean stare, but really a sweetie once you get to know him. Laugh a minute jokester ... but the joke was on us.

Donald Dump – Former real estate typhoon, turned self promoting celebrity  with a biq quaff of hair who specializes in arm candy and self dealing on his own reality TV show, "Your Fired." Brought new levels of disingenuouslness to the Miss America Pageant and the Mr. America presidential sweepstakes. But we will say this about him: he can produce his own birth certificate.

Donald Dumbsfeld – Former Dork of Defense who mastered the art of answering his own questions when asked something else. But he really was the engineer of the War we didn't want to fight. He is a fighter ducking questions tossed like bombs in his face, but an intellectual wimp when having to defend what he did in Iraq.

Foxy News Network - Fair and balanced news ... totally …. yeah … right ... largely without substance, but still the rabid right devours their brand of junkfood journalism as if it were tasty morsels of news McNuggets.

Huck Mukabee – Darling of the religious right, but what a name. Parody

ripe ... right out of the gate. Pastor like and religiously oriented person, but what exactly is he preaching on Foxey News these days. Attacks Democraps like it's a holy war. Maybe it is.

Glen Beek - Ultra dramatic radio personality and Foxey News Commentator now turned empire builder and rally organizer.

Jeb P. Wush - Helped seal his brother's victory ... the greatest heist in human history? (See The Book of Jeb, preceding)

Jerry Foulmouth – Religious Wrong figurehead and poster child for foot-in-mouth disease.

John Boner – Straight up guy. Passionately believes in small but erect government. His strength: tactical insertions of semenal clauses into the wide open spaces of Congressional legislation. A real comer.

John McPain – Maverick Repugnicant Senator from Arizona catapulted Saint Sarah into fame and literary torture with his pick as VEEP. The two developed a lovingly testy relationship that mirrors the love-hate relationship of all Repugnicants with their logic.

Jon Stuntman – Daredevil ex-governor from Utah who bravely strode unarmed across enemy lines into the Obama administration as ambassador to China. His billionaire daddy, made his money selling Styrofoam hamburger containers to MacDonalds, all of which sit serenely today in landfills across the country and won't decompose for 500 years. Young John now surveys the rubble left by the other Presidential contenders, wondering, "Where's the beef?"

Karl Rude – A Repugnicant once so revered he became self-appointed White House etiquette expert and political strategist. Today losing credibility with Repugnicance ... unfortunately he sometimes lapses into truthtelling; once the most powerful and least accountable non-elected official ever in the history of the world, not counting Jesus Christ, of course!!!! But he more recently has gone off the deep end with his cutting remarks about Donald Dump. How dare he criticize "The Donald."

Koke Brothers – Money moves mountains, behind the scenes flowing freely from these savvy businessmen pulling the strings of political puppetry.

Michael Stole - Former Chairman, Repugnicant National Committee - Special expertise is spending money that isn't his ... lavishly.

Mitch McConman – Repugnicant Senator from Kentucky who can always be counted on to deliver the conservative goods to campaign contributors.

Merciful Reynolds - Ultra-generous financial backer to George B. Wush 'n Wush Enterprises and campaign contributor to related political campaigns

Orrin Natch – Repugnicant Senator from Utah who reportedly turned the tide against locusts and liberals but still must be considered a profit of Repugnicance because he is part of the old boy Senate network just says "no" to everything Democrapic in the Washington swampland of political pork barrels and budget deficits.

Pat Blobberson – TV Evangelist and Star of the Rapturously Repugnicant Syndicated Show; penchant for making over-the-top statements; claims to have a hot line to God. Millions believe him.

Ralph Cheese – Former leader of Religious Wrong turned power consultant and Repugnicant power player. To busy lobbying now to praise God.

Robert Pinepple – Political Personality who became a Viagra pitchperson; some "older" Americans might also remember him as former Senator and Repugnicant Presidential candidate. What is he doing now? Beats us. Probably a lobbyist for pineapple juice special interests… whatever?

Rush Bimbo – Ultra heavyweight radio talk show host who seems to have discovered the right weight control drugs and the wrong political philosophy

Tim Plenty – Plenty to like about this erstwhile Repugnicant contender, but apparently the rest of the electorate never got the memo.

MYTH BUSTED
It turns out that an asshole CAN blow smoke.
PunditKitchen.com

The All Street Journal – The Mouthpiece of Repugnicance. Rupport Murdork's little baby … Financial journalism for the masses of corporate CEOs and pension fund managers … suddenly on the ropes… as the Occupy Movement puts them on the defensive. Nevertheless still championing the values that made us great as a nation of market driven obsessors and debt ridden consumers.

Snoot Gingrich Debates Newt Gangrene

NEWT GINGRICH WAS THE ONLY VIABLE CANDIDATE TO ACCEPT DONALD DUMP'S INVITATION TO DEBATE IN LAS VEGAS. THE DEBATE WAS EVENTUALLY CANCELLED FOR LACK OF INTEREST. BUT WHAT MIGHT HAVE HAPPENED IF NEWT HAD DEBATED HIMSELF WITH DONALD DUMP MODERATING? HERE'S THE REPUGNICANCE TAKE ON THIS EPIC EVENT, WITH NEWT GANGRENE GOING MANO-A-MANO AGAINST SNOOT GINGRICH.

Donald Dump: Welcome to the Presidential Donald Dump debate. First off let's talk about me. As you know, if you've read the recent Forbes article on me, I'm now worth over $7 billon dollars. I have properties all over the world so obviously that qualifies me to understand foreign policy. As to my assets, I've got a huge portfolio of property. … a wife 38 years younger than me and hot hot hot… and…

Snoot Gingrich: Donald, hello? This is our debate. You're not the only inflated ego in this room ... Remember …. You're the moderator. … moderators ask questions … is there a question?

Donald Dump: Excuse me I'm talking. I was just getting around to the questions, but first, I'd like to show some pictures of my house in Florida … it has more rooms than the White House and … Oh yes, did I mention my net worth … $7 billion ... That's billion with a capital B. and more zeros ... after it than most American's can count..

Newt Gangrene: Donald, the biggest zero is sitting right there in that chair … yes ... the one you're sitting in…. questions Donald ... ask a question ….

Donald Dump: Excuse me... Okay ... First question ... for you Snoot ... "Why you think I'm is so successful?"

Snoot Gingrich: (Sigh) ... Ask a real question ....

Donald Dump: Okay, if you have nothing to say then we'll talk about me ... again .... a talk about me. ... talk about me... talk about me ...

Newt Gangrene: We're leaving ...

Donald Dump: The doors are locked ... You can't leave ... Besides ... I just thought of a question .... My question is about education and jobs ... Snoot ... this idea you've floated where students as young as 9 years old should be put to work cleaning toilets as an assistant janitor in their schools. What's the basic idea here?

Snoot Gingrich: The problem is that most of these kids grow up not knowing what work is all about. They don't develop a work ethic and so they're totally unprepared to be productive members of society. My proposal is a way to enable them to earn some income while helping to keep the bathrooms clean and develop a fondness of work.

Donald Dump: Let me get this straight ... an inner city kid is really going to become fond of working when his only work experience is cleaning up the shit of his fellow students. Snoot ... now don't take this the wrong way ... but ... get your head on straight. Not everything that comes calling on your overactive mind should come out of your mouth. If your going to be President you've got to learn to police your own thoughts.

Newt Gangrene: Well Snoot … I think the Dumpster make a good point …

Snoot Gingrich: Look at the facts. I've written 24 books and been a college professor. I resent the notion that I can't police my own thoughts.

Newt Gangrene: I'm sorry to say this but you really do have to control your vast intelligence! Some people … the ignorant people … think you're just an arrogant snoot … those smelly protesters don't want some patrician politician, who makes $60,000 a day in speaking fees, telling some kid that he's got to get down on his knees and scrub floors for 8 bucks an hour. The question you really need to explain is, "Why your intelligence makes your time is worth almost 1000 times more than someone else?

Donald Dump: I can explain that. Bottom line: some of us are just smarter than the rest of the little people. We deserve to be paid what we're worth.

Snoot Gingrich: Exactly, the market doesn't lie. If the market for my advice is $60,000 an hour then the market knows best.

Donald Dump: I agree. The market is always right. Why I remember when the value of some of my real estate properties was …

Snoot Gingrich: Donald, this is our debate. We're running for President, you're not …. People don't want to hear your half baked ideas ….

Newt Gangrene: I agree with Snoot on this one. Donald … shut up.

Donald Dump: Don't tell me to shut up. I paid for this debate. If I want to open my mouth I will. Besides who says I'm not running for President?

Snoot Gingrich: You did… Dump … You announced months ago that while the ratings for the apprentice … were …

Newt Gangrene: Pardon me for interrupting … I think it's totally inappropriate for you to base your decision on whether or not you're going to run on the ratings of your TV show.

Donald Dump: Hold it guys…. There are bigger issues at stake here. If no candidate emerges who is strong enough to beat Obama in November than I'm completely justified in keeping my options open … If I need to run to save this country from Obama then I will.

Snoot Gingrich: Yeah and like you've got a real chance of beating Obama. Your poll numbers were in the Dumpster?

Newt Gangrene: Snoot … you should talk… just a few months ago your campaign was dead in the water.

Donald Dump: Gentlemen … you're supposed to be debating each other. … not me. Let's move on...

Snoot Gingrich: I don't want to move on before I've had a chance to respond to Newt. Tell me Newt… what were your poll numbers a few months ago?

Newt Gangrene: I'm running a positive campaign. Let's not dwell on negatives here. The good news is that I'm now leading the pack. For that we can, primarily, all thank ourselves and our enormous egos.

Donald Dump: Yes, good point … and now … we've got to get this debate back on track. Snoot what is your position on Libya?

Snoot Gingrich: We shouldn't even be talking about Libya when we can't even govern our own country. Congress is in stalemate … Democraps and Repugnicants are at each others throats, meanwhile our credit rating as a nation has been downgraded … we have become shrill. …

Newt Gangrene: And Snoot, tell the people how things were different when you were Speaker of the House.

Snoot Gingrich: When I was Speaker of the House, I engineered a complete turnaround in government with the Contract With America.

Donald Dump: Yeah and in the process you alienated most of your colleagues in the House. Everybody was so pissed at you that you they initiated an ethics investigation that consumed government and wasted millions of dollars of taxpayers money … why … all it produced was acrimony and hundreds of thousands of pages of gibberish.

Snoot Gingrich: Gibberish it was … I was almost completely exonerated. It was a capriciously political witch hunt. I did nothing wrong.

Donald Dump: Then why were you fined $300,000 for your wrongdoing?

Newt Gangrene: Hey guys, we need a little financial perspective here. $300,000 is chump change in comparison to all the money Snoot took in through lobbying. It was worth it both from Snoot's perspective and the lobbyists. A good investment all around.

Snoot Gangrene: Exactly it was a really good investment. The health care lobbyist good a great return.

Newt Gangrene: And remember, I wasn't lobbying. I was proffering advice.

Snoot Gingrich: It was great advice too. The advice you gave to Fannie Mae, for a cool $30,000 ... by the way ... what did you tell them that was worth all you got paid?

Newt Gangrene: I told them all the things that they shouldn't do ... but they still did it.

Snoot Gingrich: So they must have really valued your advice ... if they ignored it.

Newt Gangrene: Yes and remember, as a consultant, I can only offer advice. I can't tell them what to do. Those are the limitations of being a consultant.

Snoot Gingrich: Precisely, at least we can agree on that point and when I'm elected President, I will no longer be a consultant so I can start implementing all the things that I have told others not to do, when I was a consultant.

Newt Gangrene: Well put Snoot! We're all on the same page now.

Snit Romney Debates Mutt Romnoid

Well, that was enlightening. Pushing ahead precariously through the Republican Babble, here's the repugnicant Debate between Mutt Romnoid and Snit Romney.

Snit Romney: Anybody who has watched the Republican debates knows that your big problem is that the two sides of your own mouth don't talk to each other enough. Mutt, to be perfectly blunt, your multiple personalities

have a communication problem with each other.

Mutt Romnoid: Listen Snit, I don't have multiple personalities. I am who I am, a man of constancy. And I'm candidate is the best qualified to be President, because I've been in business my whole life, except for the part of my life when I was in office.

Snit Romney: Wait you're right. I forgot …. You don't have multiple personalities. You don't even have one personality. You're nothing but a political robot masquerading as a candidate. You've been programmed by your handlers to say anything that might appeal to whoever you're talking to at the moment.

Mutt Romnoid: You should talk. Everybody knows that Snit Romney is the most irascible and irritable candidate in the race. Snit Romney takes offense at the smallest slight. His skin isn't thick enough to endure political mudslinging. That's what running for the Presidency is all about.

Snit Romney: Mutt, you should talk. You're nothing but an intellectual mongrel. Your positions are all over the map. In Iowa and other conservative states cast yourself as a conservative of convenience, but in your home state of Massachusetts, your almost a Dukakis liberal. Do you have any core convictions that carry over from one constituency to another?

Mutt Romnoid: You just proved my point. As soon as I started attacking you, you had a snit. You went at me with a personal attack, instead of addressing the issues I raised. I'll ask my question again, "Do you have any core convictions?

Snit Romney: Of course I have core convictions. My positions on lot's of issues have been consistent … too many consistent positions to list in all their variety. I'm a man of stability, care and constancy. For example, I've been married to the same woman for 40 years. No wait, I've only been married to her for 17 years.

Mutt Romnoid: What did I just say?

Snit Romney: Omigod, you're right. I can't even agree with myself on how long I've been married to my wife.

Mutt Romnoid: No worries Snit. The details are insignificant … The important point is that you've been married to the same woman, no matter how long it was. Not like other serial adulterers in this race. But back to you … Snit, you have said that you are totally opposed to Obama Care, but in your book you wrote that you supported the Health Care legislation in Massachusetts that could become a national model.

Snit Romney: Wait I'm confused. Are you for the individual mandate or against it. If you're against it, why is it the law in Massachusetts?

Mutt Romnoid: I'm 100% opposed to Obama Care. It's a disaster. … and I've been consistent about that position for a long time … at least as far back as the last time I changed my thinking about it. Obama Care going to add trillions to the national debt at a time when we can least afford it. I knew it would be a disaster and I never would have supported the national legislation or anything of the kind.

Snit Romney: That is total BS. Obama Care has some good things in it. The parts of it that are consistent with what we did in Massachusetts are based on sound thinking. We need to find a way to provide health coverage to the millions of American's who today are not covered, but they shouldn't have to pay for it. When they get sick, we all have to pay for their care. That's just not fair to the rest of us.

Mutt Romnoid: So there you go again ... that's what you wrote in your book, until you changed it?

Snit Romney: You brought that up before. I've read my book. In fact I wrote my book. I know what's in it and I didn't come out for the individual mandate.

Mutt Romnoid: Listen Snit. I read your book. It was in there when it came out in the hardcover edition of the book, but you took it out of the paperback.

Snit Romney: $10,000 says you're wrong.

Mutt Romnoid: I'll take that bet and bump you $20,000.

Snit Romney: Okay, I'll bump you another $20,000. Hey 50 grand is chump change to me. I've been in business and I've been successful. I've got a ton of dough. I know how the economy works. It's all just a big game, with a lot of betting going between the deals. I won most of my bets and I'll win this one.

HUMANOIDS FOR ROMNOID

Mutt Romnoid: You're on. Let's shake on it. We'll let Rick Perry decide who's right on this.

Snit Romney: Hold it right there. P.Rick Perry doesn't know his ass from his elbow. He can't even remember three reasons he's running for office. How can he remember what he read in my book years ago?

Mutt Romnoid: There you go again … having a snit about P.Rick Perry. What about this outrageous claim you keep making that you're not a career politician. The only reason you're not is that you lost to Ted Kennedy for Senate in 1994.

Snit Romney: The only reason, I lost to Ted Kennedy because my positions weren't liberal enough for Massachusetts voters. I've learned my lesson, and my positions are more finely calibrated now.

Mutt Romnoid: Finely calibrated … that's a cover for a flip flop, if I've ever heard one … calibrated so that they can be cast as conservative when it's convenient. I know you like fudge, but …

Snit Romney: Listen, Mutt…. I'm a businessman. Businessmen are conservative. I was in the venture capital business and the capital we invested was the engine of growth … we stimulate jobs by investing in America's future.

Mutt Romnoid: That is total BS. As a venture capitalist you bought companies, fired the workers … stripped them down to their core competencies and never thought twice about how your moves as an investor impacted the lives of the people you put out of work.

Snit Romney: The people we put out on the street, had become unproductive in their current jobs. Much better for them to hit bottom, then retool themselves so that they could become more productive in other

companies and other industries. That's how the economy works.

Mutt Romnoid: That's what scares me about you Snit. You say you know how the economy works, but you only know how it works for you and your fellow investors. You know how to use the rules of capitalism to benefit the investor class. You place your bets on companies....

Snit Romney: Mutt you brought that up before. $10,000 says I know how the economy works ... are you on?

Mutt Romnoid: You're on ... and we'll let the voters decide about this one.

ROBOTS FOR MITT ROMNOID

TALKING POINTS: Repugnicance is going viral. Use these links as touchstones to the rapture.

REPUGNICANCE ON FACEBOOK

HTTP://WWW.FACEBOOK.COM/PAGES/
REPUGNICANCE/332293770120032

REPUGNICANCE ON TWITTER
@REPUGNICANCE

REPUGNICANCE ON GOOGLE+

HTTPS://PLUS.GOOGLE.COM/B/
108445014202924877393/

About the Author - George Won't

George Won't is the anthesis of George Will. George Will writes for the bastion of the political establishment, *The Washington Post*. George Won't scribbles at the armory of political irreverence, *The Washington Pissed*.

George Will is the consummate Washington insider. George Won't is the ultimate political outsider.

George Will is the master of syntax and grammatical etiquette. George Won't don't give a rats ass about choosing politically correct words. Fact is George Won't don't even care about proper spelling, periods, commas and other etraneous punctuals.

George Will was educated in the Ivy League and circulates with aplomb through Washington society circles. George Won't picked up what he knows at Avery's Barber Shop on Fourth Street. "Hell no!"... You'll never see him wearing a tux, 'n you'll never see George Won't sittin' with the power elite at DC dinner parties. George Will wears bowties ... George Won't don't wear no ties.

At Georgetown parties George Will knows how to hold utensils all prim and proper. He daintily picks up food for thought and skillfully inserts choice morsels of gossip into his widely read columns.

George Won't stuffs food in his mouth with his fingers just like the rest of the locals at the Squat and Gobble in Paint Creek, just outside of town. He listens good to what common folk is saying and somehow works it into wordage that nobody will cherish forever. Don't forget to read the companion book, George Won't authoritative work on the Republican Religion entitled: *Repugnicance: The 2012 Version of the Republican ~~Bible~~ Babble*. Whatever?

Repugnicance

The 2012 Version of the Republican Bible Babble

Edited and Curated by

George Won't
Columnist for the *Washington Pissed*